"Everyone Helped His Neighbor"
Memories of
Nags Head Woods

by
Lu Ann Jones
and
Amy Glass

North Carolina

ISBN 978-1-4696-5001-2 (alk. paper)
ISBN 978-1-4696-5002-9 (ebook)

Research and publication of the original document was
made possible through grants from The North Carolina
Humanities Committee, a state based program of the The
National Endowment for the Humanities and The Outer
Banks Community Foundation in association with The Nature
Conservancy.

No part of this document shall be considered as representing
the views of The North Carolina Humanities Committee, The
National Endowment for the Humanities, The Outer Banks
Community Foundation, or The Nature Conservancy.

Release forms for all interviews are on file at Nags Head
Woods Preserve, Kill Devil Hills, North Carolina. Design and
Typography of the original edition: Bruce W. Whipple.

For more information about The Nature Conservancy or the
Nags Head Woods Preserve visit www.nature.org.

WOODS. NAGS HEAD. N. C.

ACKNOWLEDGMENTS

The authors wish to thank several people who helped make the Nags Head Woods Oral History Project a pleasant task. The narrators of this book welcomed us into their homes and were generous with their time and memories. Learning by listening to them was a delight.

During the field work Jim and Henrietta List, Vera and Upshur Evans, Kathryn Howd, Belle Lanier, and Helen Hill Miller shared hospitality, food and shelter. Frances Inglis of Edenton, North Carolina, led us to several good sources.

Archivists and reference librarians at the University of North Carolina at Chapel Hill made the research easier. Alice Cotten of the North Carolina Collection was particularly helpful. Jerry Cotten, photographic archivist at UNC's Wilson Library, located many of the historical photographs included in this booklet.

Catherine Bishir of the Historic Preservation Section of the N. C. Division of Archives and History made excellent comments on early drafts of the manuscript. Jacquelyn Hall, director of the Southern Oral History Program at UNC guided us all along the way. We, of course, are responsible for any flaws that remain.

Lu Ann Jones

Amy Glass

CONTENTS

Foreword

By David Cecelski, February 22, 2018

I am deeply honored to have been asked to say a few words about this wonderful new edition of *"Everyone Helped His Neighbor": Memories of Nags Head Woods*. I grew up on the North Carolina coast and I have been devoted to preserving its history and telling its stories all my life. Lu Ann Jones and Amy Glass's book has long been one of my guiding lights and belongs on the shelf of every Outer Banks lover's library.

First published by The Nature Conservancy in 1987, this wise and captivating book was a revelation to those of us who cherish the Outer Banks. Through the voices of Nags Head Woods' last residents, we came to see and understand the Outer Banks as we never had before.

This book tells a remarkable story. For untold generations, the community of Nags Head Woods flourished on the sound side of Bodie Island, a long, narrow stretch of sand dunes, salt marsh and maritime forest that makes up one of the northern Outer Banks.

On those shores, the Wright brothers made their first flight. Legendary lifesaving crews braved gales and surf to rescue shipwrecked souls. And to this day, you will still find some of the most beautiful wildlife refuges and seashores in America there.

But long before the Wright brothers—and long before any bridge or paved road brought vacation goers and retirees to the Outer Banks—Nags Head Woods was home to a close-knit, salt-drenched community of fishing, farming, and waterfowl hunting families that lived nestled between two great sand dunes, Jockey's Ridge and Run Hill.

To outsiders, Nags Head Woods felt like the end of the world. The broad waters of Roanoke Sound lay to the west, the Atlantic Ocean to the east, with no bridges to the mainland until the 1920s and the community's fate tied to a breathtakingly beautiful, but often perilous sea.

Like the ancient live oaks that sheltered the little settlement, the people of Nags Head Woods bent when necessary, adapting to storms and changing times alike, but they kept their roots deep in the soil and stood strong and steadfast.

Through good times and bad, they made a home in that one part of the island where the dunes towered high enough to shelter their farms and gardens from the salt air and the great storms.

This is their story. And we are lucky to have such gifted storytellers. Lu Ann Jones and Amy Glass are both extraordinary oral historians, trained at the

Southern Oral History Program, the University of North Carolina at Chapel Hill's groundbreaking center that is dedicated to preserving the stories of all those forgotten by history.

Together they sought out Nags Head Woods' last residents. The island settlement had gradually declined in the early 20th century and had faded away by 1950, but the two young historians located many of the last people who had grown up on those shores.

They visited and talked about the island's history. They listened to stories about childhoods, living off the land and sea, and what the Outer Banks was like before the oceanfront developments and the crowds of visitors discovered the island.

They talked about hurricanes, shipwrecks, and a simpler way of life. The islanders told them how they used to haul fishing nets on the ocean beach long after the sun had set, and the beauty of those moonlit nights.

They described plush times, like during the sturgeon fishery's heyday, when a steady traffic of boats carried the fish's roe—caviar!—as far as Philadelphia and New York City.

And they remembered the hard times, like the years during the Great Depression when Ester Tillett Beacham saw her mother working herself to the bone. "She worked constantly," she told this book's authors. "She was so tired some nights she didn't even want to take a bath. Some afternoons she would ask me to draw a pan of water for her to soak her feet in."

Even in hard times, the people of Nags Head Woods clung to Bodie Island as long as they could. And their words remind us that we can find a path forward in our own hard times, too.

As another Nags Head Wooder, Vandelia Brown, remembered, "Our neighborhood helped each other in times of distress. We found love and concern in sickness and death."

When this book first appeared 30 years ago, I thought it was a groundbreaking approach to telling the story of the Outer Banks—and I still think so today. Lu Ann Jones and Amy Glass continue to inspire us by their extensive use of oral histories and by the quiet, but determined way that they place the island's women at the heart of Outer Banks history.

Of course, a lot has changed on the Outer Banks even in the three decades since *"Everyone Helped His Neighbor"* was first published.

Unfortunately, few of the islanders who shared their stories with Lu Ann Jones and Amy Glass remain with us. Time has passed. The memory of Nags Head Woods has dimmed further.

Yet the voices that you will hear in this book are as fresh and relevant today as they ever were—and their stories have only grown more precious.

I recommend that you find a front porch. Sit a spell. Look out on the sea or the salt marsh and spend some time with the people of Nags Head Woods.

Better yet, visit the Nags Head Woods Ecological Preserve, which includes much of the old village's forests, marshes, and ponds. Take this lovely book with you and read it to yourself or read it aloud with family and friends.

See the community of Nags Head Woods come to life again. Get to know the history of the Outer Banks in a deep-down way for the first time. Listen to the voices.

INTRODUCTION

Nags Head Woods, home to a unique array of plants and animals, was also until the twentieth century home to about forty families. To learn more about the social and cultural history of this community, the Nags Head Woods Ecological Preserve in the summer of 1986 sponsored interviews with people who once lived in the Woods or visited often. Funding from the North Carolina Humanities Committee and the Outer Banks Community Foundation made the project possible.

Among the questions asked were: How did the physical environment shape the lives of Woods people? How did residents make a living? How did they raise families and forge a community? How did they tend to their medical needs? What means of transportation and communication did they use? What did they do for recreation?

Brief introductions to the people who helped answer these questions are in order.

Marshall Field Tillett, *age 84, the son of Tilghman and Harriett Baum Tillett, lives in Nags Head and still farms the family homestead in the Woods.*

Lu Ann Jones and Marshall Tillett, 1986

4

Boone Tillett, ca. 1970

Ester Beacham, 1986

Boone Tillett and Ester Beacham *are the children of Maggie and Erb Tillett. Mr. Tillett, a practicing attorney at the age of 93, lives in Blackstone, Virginia. Mrs. Beacham has returned from Arlington, Virginia to live in Kitty Hawk.*

Vandelia Tillett Brown, *sister of Marshall, lives in Zebulon, North Carolina. In place of an interview, Mrs. Brown shared her memories in a long letter.*

5

Norris Austin, 1986

Norris Austin
is the grandson of Maggie
and Erb Tillett. He is postmaster of Corolla, NC
and an active Preserve volunteer who has refurbished
a family cemetery in the
Woods.

Evelyn Wise Gray,
daughter of John and
Mary Wise, grew up in
the Woods. After living in
many parts of the country,
she and her husband
moved to Kill Devil Hills
following his retirement
from the Coast Guard.

Evelyn Gray, 1986

Leland Tillett, 1986

Leland Tillett
is the cousin of Marshall Tillett. His father was born in the Woods, and Leland was a frequent visitor.

Sylvia Culpepper
was born in Wanchese and joined the Woods community in 1923 when she married Hal Wood Culpepper. She now lives in Nags Head.

Texie Tillett Meekins and Mildred Midgett
both grew up and still live in Wanchese but visited relatives and friends in the Woods.

David Lawrence
was a newcomer to Dare County in the 1920s. He now lives in Kitty Hawk.

Sylvia Culpepper and LuAnn Jones, 1986

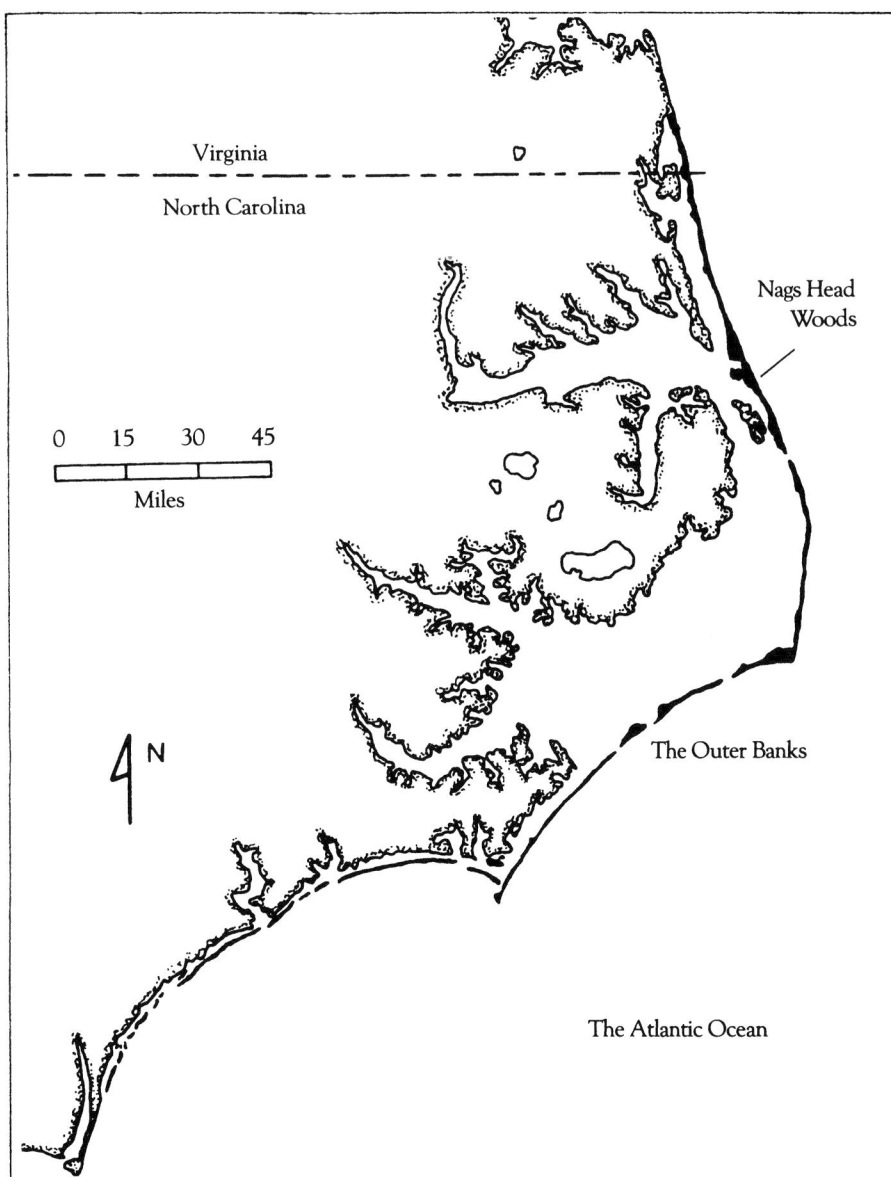

Virginia

North Carolina

Nags Head
Woods

0   15   30   45

Miles

N

The Outer Banks

The Atlantic Ocean

The Outer Banks of North Carolina

Nags Head Woods, a maritime forest located on the sound side of Bodie Island, has an interesting natural and human history. It is a unique feature of the North Carolina Outer Banks, a string of barrier islands that stretches for 170 miles from the Virginia line to Cape Lookout. Sand dunes, or sand hills, characterize the northern Outer Banks, and Nags Head Woods is tucked between the 110-foot-high Jockey's Ridge, the tallest active dune in the eastern United States, and Run Hill, a 60-foot-high sand dune that literally "runs" to the southwest at a rate of ten feet per year. Roanoke Sound forms the western border of the Woods.

The distinguishing features of Nags Head Woods are its forested dunes and fresh-water ponds. Cresting from twenty to ninety feet above sea level, the dunes protect the Woods from the salt spray and high winds that blow in from the ocean. Nags Head Woods is therefore able to support shrubs and trees typical of Piedmont forests—pine, oak, hickory, and beech. Interspersed among the dunes are more than twenty-five fresh-water ponds. The origin of these ponds has been the subject of much research and debate. Some authorities argue that they resulted from a change in sea level over the millennia, while others claim that inlets that once existed there closed and later filled with fresh rain water. Speculation over the genesis of the ponds continues, but one thing is clear: the unique combination of forested dunes and fresh-water ponds on the sound side of Bodie Island fostered the growth of a forest that, according to one recent survey, is "better protected from the damaging effects of the ocean than any other maritime forest along the Carolina coastline." (Otte, 1984)

9

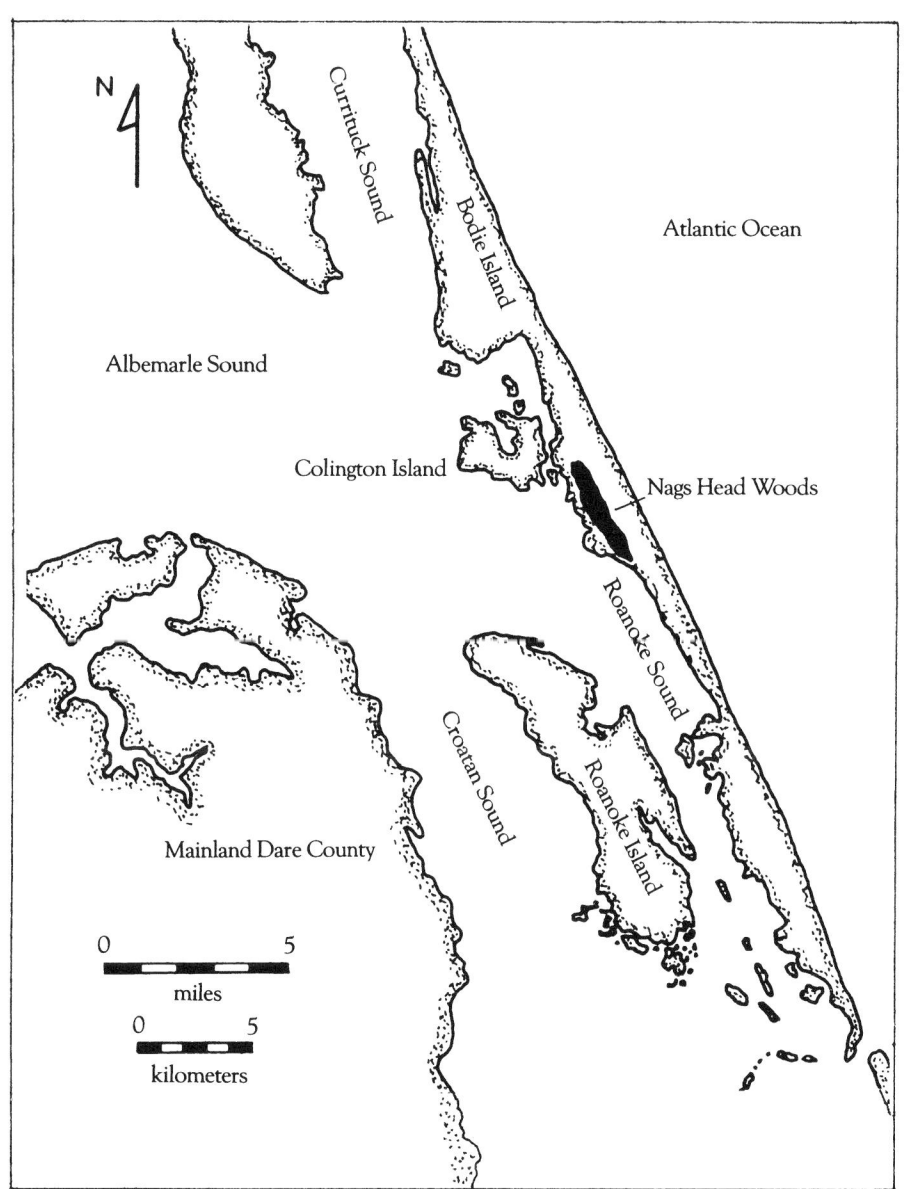

Nags Head Woods offered protection for people as well. Although little is known about the first people to live in the Woods, the best educated guess is that the land was inhabited by Algonquin Indians before the arrival of European explorers. By the mid-sixteenth century, the Spanish and English were making forays to the Outer Banks as they searched for a passage to the Orient. The first effort at permanent English settlement came in 1587 when a group of colonists landed on Roanoke Island, across the sound from Nags Head Woods. The group became known as the "lost colony" because of its mysterious disappearance. For nearly a century afterwards, no permanent settlements were established on the Banks. In the meantime, a successful colony took root after 1607 at Jamestown on the Chesapeake Bay, and in 1665, King Charles II granted to eight Lords Proprietors a vast territory that included what would become North Carolina.

By 1660 settlers were once again trying their luck on the Outer Banks. Most were English yeomen from the Chesapeake and Albemarle regions. While many bought land, others gained property simply by claiming squatters' rights. One hundred years later, families were obtaining land in Nags Head Woods and bequeathing it to their heirs.

These early settlers, as have successive generations, built their homesites in "hummocks," or wooded tracts slightly higher than the surrounding area. Men and women subsisted by fishing, hunting, and growing their own food. Bankers also met their needs by "wrecking," or salvaging cargo from shipwrecks. In fact, according to a popular legend, Nags Head got its name from a scheme Bankers used to lure unsuspecting ships toward shore. A pony with a lantern tied around its neck supposedly was driven up and down the beach at night; the bobbing of the light resembled the motion of a vessel in harbor and served as a deceptive beacon to captains offshore who steered their ships on a destructive course.

By the early nineteenth century, federal and state governments initiated efforts to assist shipping along the Banks' treacherous shoreline. Between 1798 and 1848, lighthouses were built on Ocracoke, Hatteras, and Bodie islands to guide ships and make the waterways safer. The North Carolina General Assembly took control of ship scavenging in 1801 when it established wreck districts and wreck masters. County courts appointed Commissioners of Wrecks to take custody of vessels that stranded along the "graveyard of the Atlantic" and to seize or auction the salvaged cargo.

Postcard

11

*Oak staves that washed ashore
from a Hatteras shipwreck—*
1900

"they didn't bother to cut the timber down 'cause it was already cut down. An old ship would drift up and they'd go on board there and tear part of the decking out, or the sills, take the old masts and carry 'em to the mills and have them sawed."

Leland Tillett

The Banks were also beginning to attract summer visitors by the early nineteenth century. Most were planters and merchants from the Albemarle region who brought their families and servants to breathe the salt air and bathe in the ocean, activities believed to ward off malaria. By 1830 summer visitors began to build small cottages on the sound side of Nags Head in or near the protective woods, and by 1838 a hotel, said to have accommodated 200 guests, was flourishing near the sound. According to one local historian, the first oceanside cottage went up in 1855. Because the ocean beaches were considered too vulnerable and dangerous, most people stayed close to the sound side of Nags Head.

In contrast to the wealthy summer people from the Albemarle, Bankers saw little reason to own slaves. This does not mean that they were unaffected by the Civil War. Union forces invaded the Banks and occupied much of the area throughout the war.

After the war the federal government continued its efforts to make the Outer Banks safer. In the late 1870s the government set up twenty-five Life Saving Stations between the Virginia line and Cape Lookout, including those established at Nags Head, Kill Devil Hills and Kitty Hawk. The Life Saving Service offered regular paid employment close to home for many male residents of the Outer Banks. By 1915 the Service had merged with the U.S. Revenue Cutter Service to form the U.S. Coast Guard.

In the early twentieth century Nags Head Woods was a thriving community. While some families lived on farms in the Woods, others clustered on its southern edge in houses perched over the sound. Children could attend a neighborhood school through the seventh grade, and Nags Head Woods supported two churches. On the Woods' southern border Graham Hollowell ran a store where residents traded and collected their mail. Visitors swelled the population during the summers.

Interviews with residents of Nags Head Woods who came of age in the first half of this century convey how much change they experienced. Boats and beach carts gave way to automobiles. Catering to the tourist trade grew from a "cottage industry" to a big business. New laws altered customary ways of raising livestock on an open range and hunting. Recreation and amusements became more commercialized and less centered on the family. Medicine became the province of professionally trained doctors rather than self-taught midwives.

Turning points for the Nags Head Woods community were World War I and the 1930s. The war drew many men into the military, and the shipyards in Norfolk, Virginia offered jobs that lured others away. As residents began to scatter, the churches declined and the Wood's school eventually closed.

Improved transportation brought other changes. Between 1928 and 1931 the construction of bridges across the Roanoke and Currituck Sounds and a highway along the beach vastly increased the flow of automobile traffic on the Outer Banks and laid the foundation for a burgeoning tourist industry. Living on the ocean side of the island also appeared less dangerous after the 1930s when the government sponsored dune building programs. Sand fences created dunes along the beach, and seedlings and shrubs served as sand binders.

This combination of factors pushed and pulled the last generation of natives out of Nags Head Woods by 1950. Today part of the Woods' unique dunes, forests and ponds are owned by The Nature Conservancy and managed as the Nags Head Woods Ecological Preserve. And part of the Woods is home to a new generation of inhabitants who live in modern condominiums, villas and cottages.

The Setting:
Nags Head Woods

Residents took advantage of Nags Head Woods' natural resources and adapted to its special features. A profusion of wild foods were available. Texie Meekins, a life-long resident of Wanchese, recalled "at a certain time of the year, my mother would go [to Nags Head Woods] for a week to pick huckleberries. So we used to haul through the Woods after huckleberries. They're smaller than the blueberries and grow up on high bushes. We took them in a bucket, and each one had to be picked individually and that little stem pulled off. They were real tiny, so you can imagine it took us quite a while. We children worked with [my mother]. Then she canned them, just like you would most any other kind of berries. They were delicious for pies in the winter."

Blackberries and grapes grew everywhere. "Blackberries were on the ground trail," Sylvia Culpepper explained, "and they came in June. Huckleberries came in May, and blackberries came in June, and we got 'em all. People'd just go out huckleberrying early in the morning. Some of 'em got full of ticks, red bugs, and everything else, but I never did." Mrs. Culpepper seemed mostly partial to the grapes. "There were all kinds. Fox grapes, and then the big blue grapes, and bunch grapes. We'd make jelly, and that's delicious. It's got a tart to it that's different from the regular. And it's good for winter time to serve with turkey and meats of the winter. Kind of a winter grape, I call it. They grew right at the edge of the sand dune. I don't know why, but the edge was full."

15

Nuts were also good eating. Chinquapins roasted in the shell were "the best things you ever ate in your life," according to Boone Tillett. Sylvia Culpepper explained that a "chinquapin is a little thing that looks like an acorn. It has a real [hard] outer hull that is just little sharp points that sticks in you and in the fall they're ready. You go in there and get 'em, and they taste like acorns. We used to eat acorns, we'd roast them. I don't think they ever use acorns for anything now, do they? We used to eat 'em. We ate everything like that. I think that's why we were healthy and never had any constipation." Culpepper and her sister-in-law also gathered hickory nuts. "We'd get us a whole bag of nuts to last us all winter. We'd make fudge and put them in. They're hard to pick out—they're like black walnuts—and we'd put them in fudge or in cakes or in cookies or in anything we could. We'd have us a big burlap bag full of hickory nuts."

The Woods also provided rich resources for seasonings, medicines, building materials, and even clothing. Leland Tillett remembered his father pointing out several old trees in the Woods. "He said, 'Son, I've skinned that old hickory nut tree many a time.' I said, 'Pop, what did you take the bark off for?' He said, 'We used to make our own leather. We'd break all that [bark] up into water and put it in there with the cow hide and it would help take the skin off and turn it red, turn the leather red.'" Dyes could be made using the brown hulls of nuts, and

pokeberries yielded a red dye. Many people used the abundant bayberry for seasoning. Sylvia Culpepper claimed "the best flavor you could ever imagine" came from adding bayberries to homemade lard.

Many residents remember the way buildings were adapted to the Woods environment. To avoid the frequent high tides and the damage they caused, most houses were built on high ridges or hills in the Woods. Leland Tillett told how "every high lump that's in Nags Head Woods has been built on at one time or another. They lived on high ridges all over the place." Evelyn Gray's family "had a two story house with a porch all the way around it. It was up on a hill, but you could look out and see the sound." Ester Beacham's home also was "on top of [a] rise." Houses were built from timber cut from the Woods or sometimes scavenged from shipwrecks. Leland Tillett recalled, "they didn't bother to cut the timber down 'cause it was already cut down. An old ship would drift up and they'd go on board there and tear part of the decking out, or the sills, take the old masts and carry 'em to the mills and have them sawed."

Builders designed houses to withstand high winds, rising tides, and storms. "Buildings are not built like they used to be," explained Sylvia Culpepper. "It's all this glass and stuff. We used to have the storm blinds and we'd pull them in and hook 'em. And they were nice; they shaded your house. When it rained, it didn't rain right in. They were painted dark green. We propped 'em out in the summer and in a storm you'd close 'em. And most of the houses were what you call a hip roof house, that's a house that has four roofs to it. [They] would stand a storm better than anything else." But shifting sands could devour even well-built houses as Texie Tillett Meekins witnessed in Nags Head Woods. "It was a two-story house, with a kitchen built out on the back. White, trimmed in green. They had to keep moving the house, because a sand hill was taking it, until they had to move it out to the water. The sand hill kept coming over on it . . . each time we'd go [for a visit] they'd have it moved."

Before the days of scientific forecasting, storm warnings were based on weather patterns, cloud formations, and wind speed and direction. As Marshall Field Tillett recalled, "[You'd just use] your own common sense and how the weather looked and what it was doing . . . when it got to the point where it was doing bad, if you had anything to help out, you used it." Ester Beacham told how you could "see thunderstorms coming, because there wasn't as much Woods and all as there is now. You could see them coming and hear them rumbling and it was dark; you could smell them before they got here."

Despite an awareness of an approaching storm, residents could do little to protect themselves. Boone Tillett once battled with a storm. "On the southwest side [of our house], the porch had posts from the roof down to the edge of the porch. And [the wind] would pick those posts up and they would go that high off of the floor. Looked like the roof was just going to flop over, but it would always come down because wind goes by flows, you know. So I stood at the front steps and guided the posts there: when it would go up, I'd hold onto it and when it would come down I'd push it down so it'd hit the porch. Come another flow of wind, up she'd go, came down. My mother came around the corner of the house (it was blowin' so hard she could hardly stand up) and said, 'Now, you go on and get in this house You're going to get hurt.' And I said, 'No, I ain't going to get hurt.' So it finally subsided."

Hurricanes and storms battered the Outer Banks. Boone Tillett recalled that "in a storm, the livestock would come to high land. Now, down at Oregon Inlet, there wasn't any high land to go to and the tides would sweep hundreds of them off in the ocean. My Uncle Tom, I expect he lost three hundred cows at one time during a storm. The wind was so hard it just blew that water right out of the Sound, right across the beach. But up here we had no fear of that because when the wind came, the cattle would try to get into the Woods, you know, and they'd beat the storm. And the hogs would come through the Woods too."

One of the most memorable storms came in the spring of 1932. Marshall Tillett recalled that it brought "hard wind and rain . . . but no great loss. It didn't damage a house over here like it would a house over [on the shore] because the trees were so protective around it." Evelyn Gray elaborated. "Up there in the Woods we didn't really know what was going on. We knew that the sound was up pretty high, but it didn't come up to our house. After it was over, we went running down the shore and we could see all the houses was washed away down there. Piles of them. But we didn't have much damage up there in the Woods."

Less fortunate was Sylvia Culpepper whose house bordered the Sound in the southern part of Nags Head Woods. During the 1932 storm she and her family "had to get out of the house. The water came up to our porch which was right deep. It was up so I would have had to swim and my husband—he was tall, he was a lot taller—and he took me and we went to the edge of the hill which wasn't very far and our car was already there, a Ford. We sat in the car and the chickens all came up and we let some of them in the car, and they [those outside] just drowned most of them. It came up so in the car that it was just going to flood us away, so we opened the car door and started walking over the sand hill, that was just past Jockey's Ridge. The wind was beating sand all over my face and legs, and oh, it was terrible."

The Erb and Maggie Tillett Homestead

The Preserve's cultural history trail passes the Tillett homestead. Ester Tillett Beacham described how her homeplace once looked.

"You know the main road where the cemetery is? We turned off and went toward the sound. We had it all fenced in and there was a big gate there with these old hinges that were made by hand. On the right hand side as you entered the gate, my mother had her little garden. And my mother had things that people didn't have down here then because she got seed catalogues. She had things like strawberries and cantaloupes and snow peas. She liked flowers and she grew all kinds. She would put her gladiola bulbs in her garden, she'd have rows of them growing to get big to put in the house. It was just a beautiful place. And I'd go pick strawberries; I loved doing that. But I thought that was the only way to eat strawberries was picking them out of the garden I really did. And I've never cared for them now in the dish as much as just picking them and eating them.

"But anyway you go on a pretty long way, up to the house and it formed just a slight hill, and the house was on top of this rise. You could see the water from the house and you got the nice breeze from the water so it was always cool. The house was two-story. It was oblong, longer than it was wide. And then [the path] started down again. The barn was farther down and they had a big barn with stalls on each end of it and it was fenced in. I'll go right on to the sound so you can get the picture.

"I don't know if you've been back and seen that big, great, huge old oak tree? That was [to] the west of where the barn was. And then you'd go farther and there's the sound. And my father had a big boat with a house on it and he had some little boats. They were pulled up there and then he'd pull them up on the land, not too far from that big oak tree. You're supposed to take them out of the water for some time to get the barnacles off of them or something.

"You remember I said there was a big gate and you entered, came up by the garden? From the garden on to the barn was planted, farmed. And the road ran right straight on from the gate to the north end of the house, and then north of that it was farmed. On the right side of the road there was a fig tree that had some little, tiny sugar figs that's so good. Then she had another one a little farther from it that was a lot smaller, but it had the big figs on it. This huge fig tree was something. And isn't it strange how fruit trees die when people leave?

"All right, then you go down a little farther. You see, there's a ridge that's not farmed on the right hand side of the road coming in toward the house right on to the barn. And the fig trees are on this little hill like the house is. You go down the hill and they have a well that you get your water out of. It wasn't a real deep one or anything. And they could get water for the livestock, you see, because it was close to the barn, or they could use it for laundry because it was midway to the house, either way.

"Get back to the house. The house faced west, toward the sound. And in front of the house [in front of the windows on the north bedroom] there was one of these mimosa trees that has those beautiful, sweet-smelling blossoms. And you could lay there and it came up to the porch and a little bit higher, and you could smell those sweet things. Also when the sun came to the mimosa trees it was 10 in the morning. So it served two purposes.

"Next to it was a silver maple. I love them. Do you know what they are? You see them all over the fields, they're sort of a white green leaf, and underneath they're silver. And the wind blows and they rustle and that was real pretty. Then beyond it was a mulberry and a wild cherry, little cherries.

"Next to the house there's an old fashioned rosebush that had the open roses, you know, and it was white. And my mother brought it from her homeplace and it had gotten four feet tall and at least twelve feet across. It was something. And that took the whole end in front of the kitchen, you see. And then there were steps that you could go in the porch from that way. See the porches were so cool and in the summer you sat there and you didn't get as hot. They were nice in those days when you didn't have air conditioners and those things.

"Around the back of the kitchen she had some big cacti. They would have those big yellow blooms and they'd have the big red apples on them. And, oh, they were so big and they were so thorny, but they were so pretty out there. And then her garden . . . that was Maggie's flower garden with paths in it. And you could barely get through it. Some kind of pretty. And on the outer edge of the flower garden was the black walnut tree that one of my brothers planted. It had grown and it had all these walnuts on it. And the last time I saw my father he picked me some walnuts and carried them home and then he died and I couldn't eat them. But that was very pretty.

"And off from it she had a little asparagus bed. They had all the asparagus they wanted in this little tiny bed. You see, the yard has gone out and I told you the silver maple was beyond the house, and then the big long space and then the other two trees, the cherry and the mulberry. Well, beyond that there was a smokehouse where they smoked their meats. Then on the west of that, they had a dug-in root cellar. My father grew sweet potatoes.

"All right, you go down the path, way, way down. Then the marsh came up a certain distance and off from that there was still high land where it would be opposite the barn. Now on the other side of the fence, my mother had her chicken yard and it's fenced in and she has her orchard: apples, plums, blackberries, pears. I think that's it. That went all the way down to the end of the barn and all that fence. The whole place was fenced in but the marsh came in around it and they had mallows, those beautiful mallows. I've seen them blooming up there—Marsh mallow. They grow in the marsh, but they're called mallow, sounds like 'marshmallow.' They come in pink and white and they were growing in there. I thought they were so pretty."

Courtesy of Norris Austin

Maggie and Erb Tillett—parents of Boone Tillett and Ester Beacham. ca. 1870

Methodist Church Congregation,
Nags Head Woods

"And they had one Methodist Church and the preacher came from Kitty Hawk Methodist church and he came once a month. And we had services. We had Sunday School on the other Sundays when he didn't come, for the children. For there were lots of children, many children when I was first married, the woods was full of children."

Sylvia Culpepper

Kith and Kin

In Nags Head Woods kith and kin were sources of comfort from the cradle to the grave. As in most rural communities during the early twentieth century, neighbors were likely to be related. Norris Austin explained that "Everybody was more or less kin, particularly up in the north end where my grandparents were. [There was Granddaddy's] stretch of land and then his grandfather's was below. Going north was sister Penelope Baum and then Florence Partridge and right on up the road. Everybody was kin, all up and down the road, although it was maybe five, six miles that the community was stretched out."

Large families were common. Vandelia Brown and her brother Marshall grew up in a family with ten children. So did Evelyn Wise Gray. Boone Tillett and his sister Ester Beacham, together with their six sisters and four brothers, comprised the family of Maggie L. and Erb Tillett. "My family," said Mrs. Beacham, "was a village in itself."

At home parents imparted their values to their children. Marshall Tillett's father "was pretty strict, and he wanted we boys to grow up right. He didn't smoke, and he didn't drink, and he didn't chew tobacco. And he didn't think we should either. He trained us that way. I don't smoke, don't drink, and don't chew tobacco. Never have. I haven't taken but one or two drinks of whiskey in all my life. So his training done good. He tried to train us right. Along in them days when we were young, it kind of seemed hard. And he was hard enough that I don't think we really loved him like maybe we should. But it was a good thing after we got older and we could see the good effect."

Young people courted under the watchful eyes of family and community. Vandelia Brown said most courting took place on "porch swings or walks to church . . . The young men in our neighborhood were few in my dating days, but we enjoyed their visits. Many had front rooms or parlors; others used dining rooms at night. We found a way to talk over our love affairs."

Sylvia Culpepper described the restrictions placed on her when she was courting Hal Wood Culpepper. "He'd come over [to Wanchese] to see me. I didn't come over to see him because it wasn't proper. His cousin was my best friend over in Wanchese. And she was coming over to [Nags Head Woods] to spend time because a lot of the girls liked to come over here then. It was still a nice place to go swimming and go in the ocean and go in the sound and all that. And he begged me to come over with Tara and stay a week. She was coming to stay a week. But, 'Unh-unh,' Momma would say. 'You're not going over there to that beach to stay a week.' I said, 'Well, Momma, his mother's got a great big house and she's got plenty of room. She'll take care of us.' 'Unh-unh, I want you here.' So I didn't get to come over. But he'd come over to see me and we just fell in love and got married."

Sharing and visiting were ties that bound neighbors. Marshall Tillett believed that people "were different from what they are today. They visited one another; now they don't do it. Two, three times a week, your next door neighbor would be around. In the daytime, men would come and be around where the menfolks were and talk and everything. If you had anything to do, if they knew it, they'd come and help you. Didn't expect pay for it. And nights, a lot of times the older people in the family would come and sit 'til bedtime."

Families took respite from the daily routine on the Sabbath and at holidays. Norris Austin recalled that at Grandmother Mag Tillett's house "Sunday dinner was always a feast. . . . You had collard greens and ham and roast beef and baked potatoes and mashed potatoes. It was always an abundance of each kind of food that was cooked. She always had fig preserves, which was my favorite. She had strawberries that she made preserves out of. There was always lemon meringue pies, chocolate meringue pies or chocolate cake. The clabber was always my favorite. It was on the sideboard in the dining room.

"Grandpa was a person who didn't like a lot of tommyrot or tomfoolery at the table. You ate dignified and you didn't laugh real loud and boisterous. You were expected to conduct yourself like you were at a meeting or something; you were supposed to be in order. I don't mean they didn't laugh and talk, but he just didn't want kids to get out of line."

Holidays were festive occasions. "That's what I do remember," said Ester Beacham, "because the older [children] are away and coming home, every bedroom bulging, the kids all right there in that room, you know. There were so many one time, [my mother] had a big, long chest. It was a homemade thing that she kept her blankets and winter clothes in. And I had to make a pallet on top of it. Oh, yes, [a holiday] was a big to do. And do you think that it was any problem for Mother to cook all that food? And the quantity and variety? She just went about it with no trouble and had all the fun in the world. We all did."

Christmas was special at Evelyn Wise Gray's home, too. "Oh, we thought it was wonderful. We'd hang up our stockings and we'd get an apple and an orange, two or three pieces of candy. One time I got a little chicken on wheels. Oh, I thought I was rich. . . . We had holly and mistletoe. We'd go out in the Woods and get that. Decorate the house. We had a goose. There was always plenty of fowl, goose and ducks to eat."

Besides informal ways of forging a neighborhood, there were community institutions. "We had two active churches until World War I came along," Vandelia Brown remembered. "Lots of our young folks were drafted, others went to Norfolk to work in the shipyard and other good-paying jobs, so our attendance got so few our churches went down. The Baptist [closed] first, then we all attended the Methodist until it had to close its doors. But at one time we had good services and especially good Christmas programs. My oldest sister who was a teacher led us in these, and they were enjoyed by all ages. To make money to support our Christmas programs we had old-fashioned box parties, where the women fixed boxes of lunch and fruit and the elder women cooked cakes to sell. This was fun, especially for the young dating couples."

Revivals were a time for seeing relatives as well as attending services. "In the summertime," Texie Tillett Meekins said, "we'd have revivals every few months. At that time you went by boat to get to Mann's Harbor, you went by boat to get to Nags Head, and you went by boat to get to Hatteras and Avon and all those places. Whenever there was going to be a revival it was wrote down and told and all the cousins and different people that was related came in boatloads over to spend the week for revival. It was a big time. It was a time when families—when [members that had married and] branched off in these other places—got together."

Another local institution was the Nags Head Woods school where children recited their lessons until it closed in the early 1930s. According to family legend, Leland Tillett's "dad and Uncle Titus were supposed to [have built Nags Head Woods School House] in one week. It must have been a 20 foot square house. In one week they carried the wood to the lot and built the house. And on the Saturday afternoon they gave 'em the key to the school. That was right fast wasn't it, with a hand saw?"

Vandelia Brown assessed the shortcomings and pleasures of the education it offered. "In those days only seven grades were available in our little one-room schoolhouse, where we heard everybody else's lessons as well as our own. To go beyond seven grades, we had to go to Manteo and board by the month, as there was only water travel by fish boat at that time. . . . I like to remember our last

Norris and Ottley Austin in front of Erb and Maggie Tillett home, Easter Sunday 1942.

"Sunday dinner was always a feast [at Grandmother Mag Tillett's] . . . You had collard greens and ham and roast beef and baked potatoes and mashed potatoes. It was always an abundance of each kind of food that was cooked . . . You were expected to conduct yourself like you were at a meeting or something; you were supposed to be in order. I don't mean they didn't laugh and talk, but he just didn't want kids to get out of line."

Norris Austin

years in school. We took our lunches in tin buckets, sat on the side of a hill, 'our lunch room,' to eat some of the best sausage biscuits and preserves and biscuits we have ever found.

"After lunch, we would hurry to play jump rope, bob jacks, walk on Tom Walkers, or play ball. We had various activities at play time and enjoyed them all. One year we divided in two groups. The ones who lived north of the school were called *Hog Feed Peddlers* because our fathers raised hogs, and the group living south of the school on the sound shore we called *Down Road Soft Crabbers* and we would shout at each other until we got out of sight. We got a kick out of these mean pastimes, too."

The schoolchildren's "mean pastimes" suggest that there were tensions between residents of the northern and southern Woods. But most natives testified that by working together, playing together, learning and praying together, the people of Nags Head Woods maintained their community. The friendliness impressed Sylvia Culpepper, who was a newlywed when she moved to the Woods in 1923.

Hog Killings

"The old people," Mrs. Culpepper said, "I think about them and just cry. They were the kindest, best people to me that I have ever seen. I'd never seen some of them before and they were just wonderful to me and it was lonely, you know, over there and not many people. All these old ladies would come to see me and you know, I wasn't used to being treated so good by strangers. They were just the most natural, lovely people that I have ever seen."

Vandelia Brown described how the Woods community took care of its own. "Our neighborhood helped each other in times of distress. We found love and concern in sickness and death. We had no access to undertakers in those days and my daddy was called to help out. He even made caskets. Mother padded and covered them in white material to look very nice, and many times I made flower wreaths of cardboard covered with evergreens—mostly cedar and mums or any flowers available. This was my contribution to help.

"My dad had a special cart he used to take bodies to the graves on. He usually dressed the men, and Mother did the women and children. As compared to today, it was very simple. Some of our laymen would read the Bible and pray and three or four women would sing a song or two. [That] was our burial service. This is [the] best we could do in our situation, and it was appreciated by the families who were our neighbors and friends. And this was all done free; nobody had to worry about the bill [like today]."

"They'd have hog killings when it got real cold, good and cold," said Sylvia Culpepper. "Usually after Christmas. Once in a while it would get cold enough before Christmas, but we wanted to be sure that this meat would keep. And then they'd invite you to a hog killing. Oh, we had the best recipe for homemade sausage. Oh, it was so much sage and so much red pepper and so much salt and pepper—just the right amount."

The farmer holding the hog killing might invite as many as a dozen neighbors, and each had a job to do. "We'd get up real early and get our aprons and all ready. Get our hair fixed good so it wouldn't be flying around. The men would have the hogs killed. The men had scalded the hog in a big, hog-killing pot, I called it. You've seen these big iron pots. You scalded the hog in that and you scrape him down and get everything [off] and he's just as white and beautiful. Every bit of hair off. They're clean. Wash 'em down good, just pour boiling water on them, wash them down good.

"And they would be hanging up, which is a beautiful sight. If you think pig meat's dirty, you ought to see one hanging up. He's just as white and cleaned out, and every drop of blood out.

"They would hang it from a pole that they stuck from a tree, one thing to another, and then they had these hogs all ready. They'd go out and cut up the meat and we'd be ready at the tables. Then we'd start. You'd cut up the fat and you put it in a big kettle and cook it and it makes the lard. You have to watch it closely because most people do it outside, and if the fire comes up it could catch it on fire and cause a catastrophe. It's very dangerous, and people had to be very careful. The little fat cracklings are delicious to make cornbread and biscuits. But you put bay in it. You bay it, that's what makes it taste good.

"Then you'd save out the little pieces of the lean meat and all that you're going to put in the sausage. Have a pan for that. Then you'd take [the head and ears] and clean the skins off and make souse; that is delicious. You cook the feet, too. You use every part of the hog."

Jimmy and the Bull

Neighbors could help in unusual ways as Sylvia Culpepper discovered. She was grateful for a neighbor's kindness when she discovered how the hazards of the open range complicated childcare.

"There was big bulls. And one time a bull was curved up on the edge of that sand hill and my little boy was sitting right there patting that bull, and I thought I was going to die. I said, 'Oh, my land.' And I was scared to go get him—he was a year-and-a-half old. I was afraid to go get him. These white-faced bulls, you know, I'm afraid of them more than I am of the others. I don't know why, but they scare me. And that bull was laying right there in the sun. Jimmy had on a little sunsuit, just patting this bull. And I said, 'Oh, Jimmy, come here' It wasn't far from the house. And he just [shrugged his shoulders]. . . . I said, 'Oh, Jimmy, please come here.' [He shrugged again.] He couldn't hardly talk. And he just was petting it. And I thought I was going to die, thought I cannot go up to him, and take him away from that bull. I know he would kill me if I did, 'cause I'm scared of him.

"And this old man that lived not very far up in the Woods, nice old man, he came by. (He always rescued me out of trouble.) And he said, 'What's wrong with you?' I said, 'Oh, my little boy is there with that bull.' He said, 'Well, if that bull was going to hurt him he'd have hurt him before now.' He said, 'I'll get him.' So he went right up and got him. And the bull just laid there; he didn't care."

North Carolina Collection, UNC Library at Chapel Hill

"And from there, why, that same pair of oxen he brought over here to Roanoke Island in that little shad boat and he succeeded [in] grubbing and plowing his land here."
Leland Tillett

Working in the Woods

The people of Nags Head Woods had many ways to meet their needs and earn a living. Fishing, farming, raising livestock, hunting, and catering to the tourist trade provided the primary sources of food and income. Work was a family affair, and everyone was expected to pitch in. The striking features about the economy during the first half of this century were its variety and complexity. Families usually had several ways to make ends meet, and they were often connected with trade networks all along the east coast.

Woods residents learned to work when they were children. Girls helped their mothers keep house and rear younger brothers and sisters; fathers introduced sons to farming and fishing. Evelyn Wise Gray's mother counted on her older daughters for help. "Momma was always having a baby, so the bigger ones had to help out. . . . I tended to babies

all my life. [Momma] had six girls before she had a boy. . . . She kept one of us home from school one day a week to do the washing. And that was hard work, too. You'd scrub 'em on a board."

Members of Marshall Tillett's family "all worked together. [Papa would] get up about good daylight. He was up before the sun come up. He'd go to the kitchen and build a fire. In the wintertime he'd get a fire going in the living room and get things warmed up. Then he'd get my mother up to cook breakfast. He'd call we children, 'All right, boys. Get up' . . . Just as soon as we got big enough to go 'round with him, we'd go places with him. And anything we could do, we'd do it. And he'd tell us to do it."

Day in and day out, the mothers of large families faced a housefull of chores. Boone Tillett and Ester Beacham remember their mother as an especially industrious woman who was always busy. Maggie Tillett milked three cows, hauled cow manure to her cherished flower garden, raised chickens, turkeys, ducks and geese, sewed quilts and curtains, spun yarn and knitted socks, and plowed the garden if she had to. Mrs. Beacham said her mother did "whatever needed to be done . . . She worked constantly. . . . And she was so tired some nights she didn't even want to take a bath. Some afternoons she would ask me to draw a pan of water for her to soak her feet in."

"Now, in the kitchen [momma] had a woodstove that she cooked on. But in the cupboard, she had storage as well as this oil stove that she cooked on. See, that was real fast You didn't have to wait for that stove to heat up or anything. You turned it on and you cooked. So that was for her fast cooking, you know, like breakfast or something like that. Later, with the smaller family, why she practically used it all the time."

While women's work was crucial to family maintenance, it was men's work that earned money. Commercial fishing became an important part of the Outer Banks economy after the Civil War. In 1870 fishing was the leading occupation in Dare County, with 55 percent of the population engaged in this pursuit, and it continued to be an important source of income for residents of Nags Head Woods.

Fishing for sturgeon was popular in the early twentieth century. Sturgeon roe, valued as caviar, commanded high prices. Sylvia Culpepper's father-in-law "used to sturgeon fish and made oodles of money, believe it or not" Vandelia Brown's father "caught five large sturgeon one day, and the fish and caviar sold for nineteen hundred dollars, which in those days was a mighty good catch." Boone Tillett fished for sturgeon with his brother and his father. "Caviar, way back yonder, would bring about five dollars to six dollars a pound. A big sturgeon sometimes would bring about a hundred pounds of roe. Bring them ashore, extract the roe . . . [and] then we'd ship the roe to New York. Of course, from September to June a boat went out of here every day to New York. They'd ice the fish in a box and they'd take the fish into the hold of the boats, and they'd take it to Norfolk, New York, Philadelphia. A lot of times they would take it to Norfolk and put it on a railroad. But some of the boats would go right on through to New York. They always left about dark, after everybody got their roe ashore."

Overfishing soon depleted the supply of sturgeon, but the fishermen of Nags Head Woods went after a variety of catches. "In the spring of the year," Marshall Field Tillett said, "they fished shad nets about two months, I reckon. Then, after shad fishing was over, they come over on the beach and they had what they called seines and they fished from the beach."

Mending nets was one of the fisherman's most difficult and tedious jobs. Men usually mended; women sometimes helped hang the nets, or secure them to the floats and weights that kept them positioned in the water. Mrs. Culpepper described mending nets. "It's like crocheting; if you've ever tried to patch up some crochet you know what I'm talking about. You can't do it, in fact. It's just gone. And mending net, putting a piece in, is almost as bad, you know. Because you have to make the net as you go, to hitch it up with the other part."

Marshall Tillett remembered a critical change in netmaking: "Way back years ago before they got machines to tie nets with, they tied the nets by hand. Women could do that. Some women tied so fast you couldn't hardly see their hands moving. But machines came along pretty early in my day. I don't know [exactly when], but I don't think I was more than ten or twelve years old when they got to tieing nets by machine."

By 1950 only 23 percent of the people of Dare County earned their living by fishing, and today only a small number of commercial fishermen bring in most of the fish that are sold. But former residents of Nags Head Woods remember when almost everyone did a little fishing for profit.

Raising livestock was another way to make some money as well as to feed families. The Outer Banks had supported cattle and hogs since the days of earliest settlement. Although sparse, the salt grasses provided good grazing and animals fattened on nuts on the forest floor. Until 1937 the Woods and beach were an open range where cattle and hogs roamed freely to forage for food, and fences enclosed crops. Brands on cattle and notches in the ears of hogs indicated which livestock belonged to which owner. This system, common throughout North Carolina and the South until the late nineteenth and early twentieth centuries, allowed the landless and landowners alike to raise cattle, hogs and sheep. Proponents of new laws argued that enclosure would enable farmers to raise purebred stock and protect crops against roaming animals.

Marshall Tillett described the days before the fencing requirement went into effect. "Our cattle run right out on the beach. They fed in the low bottom places where water would stand and the grass would grow in there all summer. That's where they fed, mostly. There were different types of grass; it wasn't all one kind of grass.

"The only time I ever fed them any grain would be in the early spring, along about February and March. See, all the grass would be dead. When it would get blustery cold, the cattle would leave the beach and go over to the house and look for protection, and want to get in the marsh. All you had to do was just turn them in the marsh and they'd stay in there until grass begin to spring, which was about April. When grass begin to spring, then they'd want to get out and come out on the beach.

"The grass would begin to spring up then and they'd be eating it. And it would spring in the marsh, too. I don't know, maybe the flies and mosquitoes were bad over there and made them want to come out. But at a certain time of year, they'd want to get out and come on the beach. All you had to do was turn them out, and they'd go on the beach." Hogs would "go all over the Woods. Once in a while, one would come over to the ocean and maybe find a rotten fish. But they mostly stayed in the Woods."

But the Woods changed after livestock had to be fenced. Before 1937, Tillett said "there was all kinds of acorns, and hickory nuts, and chinquapins, and grapes. And every year, all that kind of stuff would be full. Just as soon as they passed that fence law and people had to take their hogs and cattle up, why, all that went away. You can't find a hickory nut in the woods. Maybe the Lord just don't like it. You can't find a chinquapin in the woods, you can't find a hickory nut, you can't find no grapes. All of it gone."

Hunting water fowl and small birds supplemented incomes and diets. Leland Tillett remembered seasonal hunting. "In the winter we'd kill the ducks. In the summer though, those [small] birds were mighty tasty. You had to sort of skin them . . . pick 'em out like you would a quail, cut 'em right down the middle. Flatten them out good and fry them and make up some good gravy and hot biscuits. That was really famous eating."

Between 1900 and 1910 hunters killed a record numbers of fowl, but in 1913 they had to abide by new restrictions. Quotas limited the number of birds each hunter could kill; live decoys and shooting from moving or movable devices were outlawed. A 1918 law made the sale of migratory waterfowl such as ducks illegal. Again, Marshall Tillett remembered that when he was a boy "people killed fowl to make money. It won't nothing to go out and kill five hundred ducks a day. Just as soon as they passed a law that you couldn't shoot from a battery, there wasn't no way for you to go out in the sound and kill ducks, all the ducks went away. The whole business. And I've seen the time on the shore side of a night especially, there'd be five hundred or maybe more geese all along there. Now you're lucky if you even see one."

Farming was another important part of the Nags Head Woods economy. With proper fertilization, the thin soils could yield a variety of vegetables and crops. Fertilizer came from two abundantly available sources—fish and cattle. Fisherman Erb Tillett sold most of his fish, but his daughter Ester Beacham remembered "there were certain types of fish that you would catch that you don't eat, such as skate. And he didn't consider croakers edible. He would haul the fish from the beach to the garden gate where he dumped the fish until later when he'd put them to his crops for fertilizer."

Marshall Tillett, whose father had forty or fifty cattle, remembered "all the fields were boarded up, had board fence around them. In the wintertime, every evening it was our [his and his brothers'] duty just before night to go down and run those cattle up and pen them in the field. After you had them penned up for a month, it'd practically be covered with fertilizer."

Once the field was manured, plowing and planting began. Marshall Tillett continued. "Soon as spring began to come and you see the weeds and then the grass turning green, then you'd take an eight-inch plow and a horse and flat-break, we called it. It's quite different now. Now, I can plow the whole field in about three hours and a half, with a [tractor and] disc. It took a long time, then, to plow it."

In addition to raising corn and soybeans to feed the hogs, Tillett's father gardened. "Sometimes he'd raise two, three hundred bushels of sweet potatoes. And he had a big cement potato house. He'd almost fill it full. Then in the wintertime people from everywhere would come there and buy sweet potatoes by the bushel." Tilghman Tillett also loaded up his horse-drawn cart in the summer and went to the cottages of the "summer people" to peddle produce and freshly slaughtered meat. A few other men did the same.

Produce sales were only one dimension of the Nags Head Woods residents' development of a service economy for the tourist trade. In the summertime Marshall Tillett's daddy "worked in his garden, and he had cattle and he had hogs and he had sheep. He had enough cattle that he used to kill one 'most every week. He'd cut it up and sell it down at Nags Head. After I got up good size (I was only around eighteen when he died) I used to help him kill the cattle, kill the pigs. Sometimes he'd kill four, five pigs every week.

"He didn't keep it. [He sold it to] all the houses and people that were living here on the shore side and a few over on the beach. He'd kill it about this time of evening [dusk], and hang it up and let it dry out in the night. Next morning he would cut it up by daylight and have it ready to [deliver]. Most of the time he'd take orders and cut it according to what they wanted.

"I hated to see sheep killed. They acted so pitiful. I used to help him kill. Had a big white mulberry tree where he done his slaughtering, the cattle and the sheep. He'd take those lambs or sheep out underneath the tree and put a rope around one foot, and kind of lift it up, and lay his head right on the chopping block, take the axe and just chop his head off. I didn't like it."

North Carolina Collection, UNC Library at Chapel Hill

ca. 1900

"Way back years ago before they got machines to tie nets with, they tied the nets by hand. Women could do that. Some women tied so fast you couldn't hardly see their hands moving."

Marshall Tillett

North Carolina Collection, UNC Library at Chapel Hill

. . . "We used to kill those by the gunneysack full. Take an old sack that you used to carry corn around, put it over your back empty, take a gun and five or six shells and you could probably go down to the pond and kill a complete sack full in four or five shots. Also birds like yellow shanks, brown backs and willets, all that type that is non-existent today" . . .

Leland Tillett

Boone Tillett's family ran a similar enterprise. "My father and the children would go out and pick snap beans, and cantaloupe, and watermelons and Irish potatoes (sweet potatoes would come in the fall), and Momma raised some frying size chickens. So they'd load up a cart, or maybe two carts, and go down the beach and stop house to house. Sell that, and come home."

After he married in 1923, Marshall Tillett and his wife continued to supply food to the summer people. "We done some farming on a small scale. . . . After I was married a while, I did a lot of killing hogs and cattle of my own. Most of the time we'd raise about a thousand chickens and sell them all around Nags Head. We weren't wholesaling them. We were retailing them. . . . Just like everybody else, we saw a chance to make a little [off the tourist trade]."

Women and girls made money by their domestic work for the summer people. Evelyn Wise Gray's mother cleaned cottages and expected her daughters to help with the wash she took in. "We'd walk all the way over to where the highway is now and carry them clothes on our back over the hills. Helped Momma wash them and stand there with an old flat iron that you heat on the stove and iron." Norris Austin said that his Grandmother Tillett also "took in washing for a while. She did the 'cottage line,' they called it."

Children also traded with the summer people to earn their own spare change and to contribute to the family economy. Evelyn Wise Gray carried on a lively business in soft-shell crabs. Vandelia Brown remembered she and her brother Marshall picked blackberries "to sell to get us a few dimes spending money."

Residents of Nags Head Woods found new ways to cater to vacationers after automobiles arrived, and bridges linked them to Roanoke Island in 1928. Some people turned their cars into a jitney service that ferried tourists from the sound side to the ocean. Mrs. Culpepper's husband delivered ice to the summer visitors. "He made a lot of money at that, too. They had a good ice plant that started up over at Wanchese. And it's the same ice plant that's to Manteo now. He started delivering ice and he carried them water. We had a pump up there on the hill that was the best water you ever saw in your life. And he'd get these big five-gallon jars and deliver it to people. All these old ladies were just crazy about him; he was really popular with the old and the young, he really was. Well, he'd sold them soft crabs when he was little and all, and he just really had it made."

Other sources of jobs and income were provided by the federal government and the military. Evelyn Gray's father, John Wise, spent his later years as a cook at the Coast Guard station. During World War I, John Wise and Erb Tillett temporarily left the Woods for work in the shipyards in Norfolk, Virginia.

Some residents like Marshall Tillett became skilled craftsmen. After he married, Tillett settled on carpentry and worked as a builder for his main source of income. "I had a chance to start in working with a contractor from Elizabeth City, Old Man [S. J.] Twine. I worked with him. The pay wasn't so big along then. We only got about forty, fifty cents an hour at that time. That was way back then in 1923, kind of depression days. Of course, pay got better all the time. We made a living. We didn't have a whole lot of money, but what money we had belonged to us and what we had belonged to us. I worked with [Mr. Twine] from 1923 until 1936. In 1936, I went in business for myself. We done all kinds of work: repair work, keeping up the houses for people, opening them up, closing them up, repairing them. Most of the time you took on new work in the fall of the year when people were away from here."

Between 1900 and 1950, the ways in which residents of Nags Head Woods earned their living became increasingly oriented towards the tourist trade. And earning a living also became more specialized. Whereas Tilghman Tillett had income from several sources that changed with the seasons of the year, his son Marshall followed one main occupation year-around and supplemented his earnings as a builder by selling produce to tourists in the summer. Then too, many Woods residents left altogether to join the Coast Guard or go to college and practice their chosen professions elsewhere.

North Carolina Collection, UNC Library at Chapel Hill

"Just as soon as they passed that fence law and people had to take their hogs and cattle up, why, all that went away. You can't find a hickory nut in the woods. Maybe the Lord just don't like it."

Marshall Tillett

39

Branding Cattle

Boone Tillett remembered the spring round-ups.

"In the spring after most of the calves were born, people here in Nags Head would get together. About fifteen of them had a pen—it was just below where Whalebone is, just about a mile right on down. They would drive everybody's cattle in a big pen down there. Then after they got them in the pen, they would put the calves in a small pen overnight. Everybody would meet the next morning and turn one calf out at a time. They might have had five hundred, but they would turn them out one at the time. And he run right to his momma. Of course, that calf hadn't had anything to eat all night, and he'd go right to his momma in a hurry. Whether the owner was there or not didn't make any difference because they could see the brands on the momma cow, and then they would brand the calf the same way. They had all the letters and numbers."

North Carolina Collection, UNC Library at Chapel Hill

The Twilight Haul

Sylvia Culpepper remembered watching her husband, Hal, and his family fishing.

"They would go fishing early in the morning and [also make] the twilight haul. That's about dark. On the beach, on the ocean, that was just beautiful. In October it was out of this world. We'd go down and make bonfires—it was getting chilly—and they'd fish. It would be just about dark. All of the families would go down there and the moon would be coming up. It was beautiful. October, it's always been my favorite time at the beach. . . .

"They'd make an early haul in the morning and then a twilight haul. But Mr. Culpepper, Hal's daddy, he'd say, 'We got to make that twilight haul.' And he had five sons and they all worked with him. They used a dory. They'd go out and set the net.

"I used to help them pick the fish out of the nets. They'd get a load of fish and they said on a moon shiny night that they would spoil. Now you could believe that; I've heard it and we did it. If the moon was shining that night, they said, 'We've got to get those fish out of the nets before morning.'

"They'd catch spot. I've seen that net so full that they looked like eggs packed in there, every mesh had a spot in it. And they'd stick in your hands and everything else, but boy, we'd get to work, we'd get those things out. . . . They'd pull [the net] right up on the shore. It lays right there and you pick the fish out, then they clean the net out, . . . and the next morning they set it again."

North Carolina Collection, UNC Library at Chapel Hill

Nags Head Fisherman,
August, 1937

41

Counting the Waves

A fisherman had to be able to "read" the ocean in order to time his boat's escape across the breakers. Boone Tillett described the practice of "counting the waves."

"There were days, maybe a week, when you couldn't go out to sea, the seas were so rough. Now I've been out lots of times with my father and he'd stand there and count the waves. 'One, two, three . . .' And then somewhere around 'eight, nine, ten, eleven, twelve' would be a little one. And he'd start over again, 'One, two, three . . .' And if the twelfth one, let's say, the next time was little too, then that was a pattern, don't you know. So he'd do that for a half an hour, maybe more."

He would stand there "right in the surf, with the boat and all ready to go. Whenever he started that series, when the eleventh wave would come, or twelfth, or whichever one he decided on, they went. Whether it was big or little, they went. They had two men in the boat with oars, and then one man—the captain—was standing at the stern of the boat, and he'd push her off in the water. Those men would start with those oars, and they go right over those waves. I've done that many a time."

North Carolina Collection, UNC Library at Chapel Hill

Peddling Crabs

Evelyn Wise Gray was an eager young entrepreneur who discovered how lucrative the soft-shell crab trade with the summer people could be.

"I'd get up mornings before day, and go lay down on a hill waiting for the soft crabs to come in, because I wanted to be the first up. . . . I'd just grab 'em; I could never do nothing with a dip net. Sneakup on 'em and feel 'em out with my toe and pick 'cm up. . . . A crab biting you, that don't bother you. Once in a while a big one would get me. But I could tell a soft one from a hard one . . . And in the afternoon when I caught all my crabs and got 'em shedded, well, I'd pack 'em in wet grass and go along, 'Wanna buy some crabs?' to every house."

Although the crabs sold for a nickle or dime a dozen, Mrs. Gray made "good money" while an adolescent. With it she bought luxuries and necessities. "After I . . . got making money at crabbing, well, I bought myself an organ. Fifty dollars. Got it from Elizabeth City. My aunt got it for me. They shipped it down on the old Trenton that come every night with supplies." She also purchased her own clothes. "[I] was the only one [in my family] who ever had any warm clothes for the winter. I had to order it from Sears, Roebuck. For weeks, seemed to me like, I'd go to the post office every morning at six o'clock to see if they'd come. Walked I don't know how many miles."

North Carolina Collection, UNC Library at Chapel Hill

"He doesn't fish for fun, he

fishes for fish."

Sylvia Culpepper

43

Getting There

In the 1920s and 1930s bridges and paved roads began to connect the communities of Dare County to the rest of the state with important consequences for residents of Nags Head Woods. Roads and bridges brought more outsiders to the Outer Banks, but natives had never been as isolated as many writers have claimed. The people of Nags Head Woods enjoyed daily mail service, and steamers linked them to Elizabeth City and more distant towns. Indeed, the people of the Woods may have been no more isolated than their rural contemporaries in North Carolina.

The water had always offered an avenue to and from the Outer Banks. According to the research that Leland Tillett has done on his family, his eighteenth-century Woods ancestors "travelled more than we ever knew. They had three or four ships.

. . . They knew more about the hurricane seasons and the winds than we'll ever know. They were smart enough that they didn't go out of Roanoke Inlet if they were going to Norfolk. They'd go fifty miles on up on the inside, go out the Currituck Inlet, dodge back in there and go up to Norfolk. They didn't travel a hundred miles outside. They had more sense than that."

Well into the twentieth century, boats, horses and carts, and walking were the primary means of transportation. Native boatbuilders adapted their designs to allow easy maneuverability in the shallow sound waters. The colorfully named "bug eyes" were sailboats with one mast. "Everybody," noted Leland Tillett, "had a long wharf or dock running out from the house and a couple of little skiffs anchored out there to a pole. They looked awful nice. Little sailboats going over to Manteo or wherever they

45

wanted to go." For Maggie Tillett hopping in her boat for a trip was as commonplace as hopping in the car to run errands is today. "She had a shove skiff that she kept up in the creek," said Norris Austin. "I've seen her once or twice go down and shove her boat out to the head of the creek and set her nets." In addition to privately owned boats, people hitched rides on the mailboat that made rounds from Nags Head to Manteo and other communities. Gasoline engines relieved boaters of their dependence on the winds. "The first gasoline engines that you could put on the boat come along about 1907," recalled Marshall Tillett. "I think [Papa] was about the second one in the county to get one of the gasoline motors. Before that they done all their boating by sailboats."

The people of Nags Head Woods used small boats for local travel and larger boats for longer journeys. "Most every fall of the year," remembered Marshall Tillett, "there used to be an old man over there in Colington that had what you call a sloop, a good big sailboat. He and maybe half a dozen men—Papa included—would take off and sail up to Elizabeth City. And they'd buy stuff up there that wasn't perishable. They'd buy sugar in a barrel—three hundred pounds to the barrel; and they'd buy flour—a hundred and ninety-six pounds to the barrel; they'd buy coffee. I remember when I went up there with them one time. Coming back from Elizabeth City, the wind shifted out to the north. That [sloop] was listed over so that the handrail on the side was over in the water. And the wind was 'Woooooo.'"

Beginning in the 1850s, steamboats from Elizabeth City, Hertford and Edenton plied the rivers and sounds of northeastern North Carolina, bringing visitors and news to Nags Head. The steamboat Trenton made runs six days a week between Elizabeth City, Manteo and Nags Head Woods, where it took on and delivered freight and passengers. In 1936 increased competition from automobile transport forced the steamer out of service. The steamers made getting to Elizabeth City, Norfolk, and points beyond simple. "We could jump on to the steamboat over here on the pier about six o'clock in the morning," said Marshall Tillett, "and go to Elizabeth City and be up there way before lunch time. Then there'd be somebody there would take you to the train, right on to Norfolk."

Besides boats, Nags Head Woods residents used horses and special carts. Leland Tillett remembered "beach carts with wide wheels so they wouldn't sink in the sand. And they had a little place down in there where you could put your feet. I used to think it was just for putting your feet. But I later found out that the cart was designed so that if the horse got into a creek or something or other and you wanted to get to the other side, then you could just direct the horse and he'd swim and pull the cart. The cart would float itself across the creek."

Daily mail service brought letters, newspapers, and magazines. Vandelia Brown remembered the trek to the post office at Graham Hollowell's store on the southern edge of the Woods. "For many years I walked to our post office—a distance of three miles—for our mail six days a week. During the [First World War] I had three brothers in service—one in the Navy, one in the Army overseas, and one in the Coast Guard—so Mother was anxious for our daily mail. Our newspaper came by mail, too. This was our only way of keeping in touch with the outside world."

Hollowell's store and the Coast Guard stations were centers of communication, and the only places with telephones until the 1940s. "One of my brothers," recalled Vandelia Brown, "was in the Coast Guard and showed me how they worked. Was the first one I ever saw, which was a curiosity to me."

Automobiles came to the Woods before adequate roads did. "I remember the first automobile that came on Nags Head," said Marshall Tillett. "It was in 1917. Melvin Culpepper bought it. But that was the first one. He just run a jitney from the shore side over to the beach—back and forth. He made some money at it." David Lawrence rode on the sandy paths as a child. In the 1920s, he recalled, there was "a ferry boat that would bring you across [from Currituck County] to the beach. Then, it was let the air out of your tires and pray. . . . We'd finally get up in the Nags Head Woods, and it was just like being in the mountains. One little old narrow trail. As a boy, I'd get carsick, the way Dad drove. The roads were just like a snake . . . One time we were going up a steep hill. Dad was going like the devil and coming up toward us was an old lady in an old pony cart. How he ever missed her,

I'll never know. Lord, save us. In those days, you looked down and [it] looked like you were looking over the edge of Niagara Falls—the mountains."

David Lawrence's father, Harry C. Lawrence was a dipper-dredge operator originally from Minnesota. He helped businessmen and politicians of Dare County plot how to develop its resort economy. Bridges and paved roads were the first steps. At the urging of Washington F. Baum of Manteo, chairman of the county commissioners, the county issued bonds to finance a bridge across Roanoke Sound which was completed in 1928. Motorists paid a toll of one dollar to use it. In 1930 a bridge spanned the Currituck Sound, replacing the ferry. The next year the state finished building the Virginia Dare Highway along the ocean, drawing residents of Nags Head Woods and vacationers alike from the sound to the Atlantic.

Roads and bridges had profound consequences. Although horses, carts, and boats did not disappear overnight, they did finally lose out to cars and trucks. Before long steamer service was obsolete and ferries were used less and less. According to Boone Tillett, "Tom Baum ran a ferry across Currituck Sound; the state came along and built a bridge. Then he ran a ferry from Whales Head across to Roanoke Island; they came along and built a bridge on there. Then he ran a ferry across Croatan Sound; they built a bridge over there. . . . Then he ran a

47

North Carolina Collection, UNC Library at Chapel Hill

"Everybody had a long wharf or dock running out from the house and a couple of little skiffs anchored out there to a pole. They looked awful nice. Little sailboats going over to Manteo or wherever they wanted to go."

Leland Tillett

48

Post Office at Colington, 1937

"For many years I walked to
our post office—a distance
of three miles—for our
mail six days a week."
Vandelia Brown

Postcard

"You'd go down to the sound. You'd follow the soundside. If it was high tide . . . it was bad traveling. If you had a car or a horse you'd take to the water."

Leland Tillett

Excursion boats at Nags Head, ca. 1915

"We could jump on to the steamboat over here on the pier about six o'clock in the morning and go to Elizabeth City and be up there way before lunch time. Then there'd be somebody there would take you to the train, right on to Norfolk."

Marshall Tillett

ferry across Oregon Inlet, and doggone if they didn't come and build a bridge there. But he didn't care. He was worth millions when he died."

David Lawrence remembered his father and Washington Baum poring over maps at night by lamplight, trying to figure out "how to open up the county. Well, they did open up the county. And look what a mess they made of it." In retrospect, Lawrence thinks his father's intentions were simple: "He just wanted to help to get the people out to find out what was going on in the world, I guess. And he wanted to keep his dredge boys busy."

To Grandmother's House

In the 1940s the trip from Norris Austin's home in Corolla to his grandparents' home in the Woods was still treacherous. **"It was a long trip from Corolla to Nags Head Woods in those days. They had a road that started where the Kitty Hawk school is now. Wasn't nothing more than just the washboard road. It was the same thing all the way to Corolla. We didn't have four-wheel drive and we were always bound to get stuck at least one time. . . . My mother would get out and push the truck while my dad drove, and we kids would play on the road or help shove.**

"The rest of the way was pretty good until you started up into Nags Head Woods itself, right on the outside of [Run Hill]. Right at the bottom of that hill was real soft. And my grandmother used to go out on Saturday afternoon and rake up pine straw and leaves on the track, and then it'd make it easier for people to drive over the hill. But by the time eight or nine of the children got home and got the tracks spun out, you'd sometimes get stuck. It'd sometimes take us three hours to get from here to Nags Head Woods. Takes maybe twenty or thirty minutes now to get there, without the tourists."

The Airplane and the Preacher

Austin's grandmother Maggie Tillett was a daring driver. Her son Herman saved money he made helping to build houses on the beach and bought his mother an automobile in the 1920s. Ester Beacham remembered, "That was the first car she ever had. . . . And you should have seen her drive it . . . You pushed it. It didn't take you, you took it."

Vandelia Brown:
"The first airplane I ever saw, I was in the church. And everyone near a window was looking out trying to see it, and I well remember what the preacher said: 'The Devil works in various ways.' I felt this was a strange remark, for us curious folks feel sure he wanted to see, too."

. . . "We'd finally get up in the Nags Head Woods, and it was just like being in the mountains. One little old narrow trail. As a boy, I'd get carsick, the way Dad drove. The roads were just like a snake . . . One time we were going up a steep hill. Dad was going like the devil and coming up toward us was an old lady in an old pony cart. How he missed her, I'll never know."
David Lawrence

In Sickness and in Health

Medical care, like many aspects of a Nags Head Woods resident's life, was a blend of the old and the new. Doctors from Manteo were available but midwives still oversaw the birth of many children. Illnesses and injuries were as likely to be treated with homemade poultices and tonics as with medicines prescribed by physicians. In Ester Beacham's opinion, "people are always running to the doctor now for things that just healed themselves then." In Texie Tillett Meekins' family, "We would go to the doctor if it was necessary, but we didn't run to one for every little thing."

Evelyn Wise Gray recalled seasonal and daily rituals. "We'd ramble the Woods, dig up sassafras, take it home and make tea. That purifies your blood in the spring. We had to take a spoonful of sulfur and molasses every morning. I hated that stuff. That was to purify your blood, too."

Home remedies answered every complaint from freckles and fevers to coughs and constipation. Boone Tillett's sisters "used to find a big old grapevine in the spring when the sap was coming up, cut a grapevine about six or eight feet from the ground, pull it over and tie it down to something. It would fill a fruit jar up overnight. That was supposed to take the freckles off. It didn't help 'em any; didn't do 'em any harm either."

If Texie Tillett Meekins had a fever, her grandmother "would go out and get a big cabbage leaf out of the garden and cool it with water from the well, and then she'd cut up some onions and different things and put in it—herbs and stuff—and bind it under your arms. It'd take the fever down . . . at least she thought it would. Yes, many old remedies that they had. Everybody had a little herb garden. My grandmother did. You went to the doctor if you were just about dead." When Evelyn Gray suffered with an earache her mother would "take a piece of salt pork, and put it on the stove and get it real hot and then jam that in my ear and that took care of that."

Routine ailments were treated at home, but serious injuries required a doctor's help. A journey to the closest physicians in Manteo or Norfolk could seem agonizingly slow. Maggie Tillett made an emergency trip across Roanoke Sound when her daughter, Virginia, was injured at a hog killing. "The pigs' feet have hoofs," explained Ester Beacham, "and [Virginia] was taking the hoof off the foot and she stuck the knife in her eye. And my mom—oh, my Lord, when I think of the things she has done—with her hand she held her eye in, while holding Virginia in her lap, in a boat, all the way to Manteo. Can you imagine that? Your own child. And so the eye was there, but she lost all the sight."

Boone Tillett recalled another accident when adequate medical care was far away. "I remember one time, a fellow was starting an engine in a boat [just] after he got the engine, and the engine backfired (you started [those engines] by hand, not self-starting) and it broke his arm. He broke it in several places. It was quite an injury. My father started with him to Norfolk in his boat and a fog came up and they didn't get to Norfolk until the next morning. They were out there all night trying to find their way, but they couldn't do it. No radios, no nothin'. In later years the government provided helicopters.

The government will come down here now and take a sick person to Norfolk on account of they can land on top of the hospital in Norfolk."

The mixture of traditional and modern medicine was especially apparent during childbirth. Well into the twentieth century, midwives were central to the care of mothers and newborns. Among the midwives who delivered babies—with or without the help of doctors—were Aunt Patty Tillett, Polly Tillett, Aunt Mave Moore, Lula Mann and Mary Ann Beasley. These women served Nags Head Woods and the neighboring communities of Manteo, Colington, and Kitty Hawk.

Midwives not only helped during labor and delivery, but joined the household before and after the birth. "When Momma was expecting a baby," recalled Boone Tillett, "why she'd tell my father, 'Well, you better go down and get Aunt Mave.' And Aunt Mave came up in a cart with my father. It might be a week or two before the baby was born, but Aunt Mave would stay around. Stay with her until the baby was about two weeks old, and by that time my mother was up [and] going around."

Sylvia Culpepper described the birth of her son. "The old midwife that helped the doctor deliver my baby lived up on the hill in a little cottage. She was the dearest thing . . . . She was Miss Mary Ann Beasley. She came just as soon as I was sick. She came and tended to me every day and she was the sweetest thing I've ever seen. She was old then, and she had learned [midwifery] from her mother. Of course, they had a lot of midwives and it went right down in the family, you know. They just took off where their mother left off. She just had good common sense. I think it was from experience.

"[When my baby was born] I had a midwife and a doctor. The doctor came and put me to sleep and that's what I thank him for, because I didn't know anything about it until I woke up. The midwife takes care of you then. She's like the nurse: she comes every morning for two weeks, I think it is. She tends to you and dresses the baby and does everything and tends to the navel cord. She came early, before the doctor could get here. My husband had to go down to Mr. [Graham] Hollowell's [store] and call Dr. Hoyle. And he had to get in his little flivver and come over here [from Manteo] and it took him quite a while."

New mothers looked to midwives and female kin and friends for advice on feeding and caring for newborns. But Sylvia Culpepper, whose mother lived in Wanchese and could not visit often, also valued the help she received from a Dare County Home Demonstration agent. "She'd come over [from Manteo] in her own car and visit me before I was ever a mother. She was just the nicest person. Then, you didn't have any baby books or anything. If it hadn't been for her, I don't know what I would do. Anything for a baby. She told me to cook his cereal for so long and I did, and he got along fine."

Using their own ingenuity, the talents of "granny women" and the skills of professionals, the residents of Nags Head Woods tapped an array of ways to care for themselves in sickness and in health.

Home Remedies

Sylvia Culpepper remembered a variety of ingenious homemade and storebought cures.

"You used simple things. You could make a good cough syrup out of honey and lemon juice, that cleared up your throat. We used alum that would dry up . . . a little ulcer or something. And we used peppermint, that's good for digestion. The peppermint candy is good for a cough, too. We used figs in winter for constipation, and they were really good. Momma would fix some preserves that weren't so much sugar in them.

"You used a collard leaf for an inflammation. If you had a sore and it started getting red all around it, Momma would say, 'Go to the garden and get a tender collard leaf, one near the bud.' So we'd go get the collard leaf. She would steam it and let the water make juices and put it on that thing. And it got well. I'm not kidding. And people used little things like that.

"They used a lot of poultices, if you had a rising or something like that that was really bad. They'd make a poultice out of cold bread and, I believe, put a little soap on it. It felt terrible, slapped on you. You know it would draw the pus out and all, and start that boil out to getting well. Get the core out of it.

"If something stung you, put some snuff on it and it'll do it, I'm not kidding. You get a yellow jacket sting you right bad and you put a lit-tle bit of snuff on it. You wet it. Momma would take some out of the box and wet it and she'd put that on there. Tobacco will do the same thing.

"We took baths in soda water. We played in the Woods a lot and got scratches and stings. We'd get this big zinc tub (we didn't have bath-tubs then so we used a big washtub) and that's what we took our baths in. Momma would take almost a handful of baking soda, sprinkle it in [the bath], and honey, it would take them places and they wouldn't even feel sore anymore.

"You know the mosquitos infect some people, some people they don't. All the children in the neighborhood would come [to my sister] and she'd get some whiskey. She wouldn't drink for anything. Hates it. She'd get camphor gum and put it in the whiskey and make her up a bottle of stuff for mosquito bites. And it was really good. The little kids used to come in every time they had a bad place and say, 'Momma, put some of your medicine on this.' And she'd daub them full. Of course, some-body'd die laughing at this stuff that we did. I'd still use these remedies today if I didn't have anything else."

Having Fun

The women, men and children of Nags Head Woods found time to have fun. Like people today, they enjoyed the natural environment. Children fashioned sleds out of oak barrels and glided down sand dunes. Folks swam in the sound, the ocean, and the Woods' fresh ponds. Hunting and fishing were popular pastimes. Some of the most common forms of entertainment were some of the simplest and centered around family and neighborhood. But as the century wore on, the developing tourist trade and inventions such as automobiles and movies also made commercial and public leisure activities available to residents of Nags Head Woods.

The Woods and the water offered myriad opportunities for fun. "Many Sundays after a Northeast storm," recalled Vandelia Tillett Brown, "we young folks would go to the sand hills and search for Indian relics. We found many arrow points and lots of pottery to show us where they had been. On our way back through the Woods we would search for wild grapes, chinquapins, acorns and black halls (a native fruit similar to a wild plum)."

When Norris Austin visited his grandparents he and his cousins built wooden boats. "We would go down on that hammock in front of the house, and we would build a little boat out of some boards. Just cut them out and nail them together. Then we stuck a rag in kerosene, put them overboard, pushed [them] off and set [them] afire. Just to watch them burn. Spend hours building them. None of us turned out to be firebugs. But it was fun for us, to make believe the boat caught on fire out in the sound."

The fresh ponds were swimming holes and fishing spots. Ester Beacham's sister Sadie "was a tomboy and she'd go up to the fresh ponds. She'd drag me along sometimes. You know, one end was real deep. She pushed me in it I learned how to swim." Leland Tillett said that the Fresh Pond was a source for "silver perch, red fin perch, chub, mullets, carp, general freshwater fish. And they was plentiful in there at times."

Norris Austin's family gathered at the ponds for fish fries. "They'd have cookers that run on kerosene and cook the fish outdoors. It was really good. They used to cook their homemade cornbread, but it was like spoonbread. You whip up the batter and fry it in the grease. Did you ever see the old kerosene stoves? They had about four burners on them. You fill it up with a gallon of kerosene and it goes down in there, 'gurgle, gurgle, gurgle.' That was what they used to cook the fish on at the fresh ponds. They'd take it all down, put it up, and you'd probably be through by dark."

Brothers and sisters were often favorite playmates. Ester Beacham remembered her brother Herman was a suitably mischievous and ingenious pal. "I wanted to tell you about [Herman's] goat," she began. "He's always been crazy about animals, was even up until he died. He had a goat and he made a little cart with wheels on it. He'd take me in the cart and drive his goat all the way to our grandfather's house—which was way down there—and back. And we'd have more fun."

One of the most common types of relaxation was visiting. Evelyn Gray remembered that "Ladies would take their young'uns and a bag of biscuits and come spend the whole day. Bag o' biscuits. [One lady] come with her two daughters and [they would] play with us. She'd sit there and talk to Momma. When they'd get hungry, they'd go in there and get 'em a biscuit.

"We'd be making doll clothes out of rags. I don't know where we got the dolls; tell you the truth, I don't remember. But we made a lot of doll clothes because we'd hide them and them two girls would come up and they'd steal my prettiest ones. Then they'd go back home. I'd go down there and steal 'em from them."

Several families owned pianos, organs or victrolas around which they gathered to sing hymns and popular songs. "We had no t.v.'s, no radios," declared Evelyn Gray, "but we did have an old phonograph, one of them with a big horn on it and little round disk things that played. I don't know [where we got it], but we had it and that was a lot of fun. We had that in the parlor; kept the parlor closed up from the rest of the kids." The organ she bought with earnings from crabbing was also a treasured source of entertainment. "I had it the first time I ever saw [my husband]. My sister was playing it and he tuned in. Boy, that was something. Run in the kitchen and tell my momma how good that man could sing."

Sometimes people gathered at a neighbor's house to enjoy music. Marshall Tillett recalled that "Old Man Adam and his family at the Coast Guard station had an old-timey phonograph. I don't know if you've seen a picture of one, with the dog listening on it. It had a horn . . . and run by springs. It didn't have flat records; it had cylinder records. They used to bring that over there to the house at night and play records until bedtime. All kinds of [music]. Some of them may have been hymns, and some of them dancing music."

By the 1920s, new bridges and roads, new technologies and the developing tourist trade affected the range of entertainment available to natives and vacationers alike. When a bridge joined Nags Head to

117. Fresh Water Lake, near Nag's Head.

North Carolina Collection, UNC Library at Chapel Hill

. . . "we'll come back up to the Fresh Pond which is in Nags Head Woods. That's the large old pond I was mentioning . . . It had considerable ducks and geese and stuff into it. And the animals used to beat around it quite a bit because, I reckon, in the summertime the grass grew better around it; it was wet."

Leland Tillett

Roanoke Island in 1928, getting to the movies in Manteo was easier. According to Sylvia Culpepper, "We'd go shop a little bit Saturday afternoon, stay over and see a movie, see all of our friends, get together because we knew everybody from Wanchese, Manteo, Colington, Kitty Hawk. They all went to movies there then because, you see, we had the road. And that road was really something to us. You see, it was somewhere to go. We liked to go somewhere else to do something. Saturday nights especially, that theater couldn't hold 'em. We'd have to stand in line and wait because it was a big thing to do."

The growing tourist trade also spurred new types of commercial entertainment. Excursion boats named Annie L. Vansciver, the Hattie Creef, and the Shultz, ferried visitors to Nags Head. Evelyn Gray remembered, "Now, Sundays, we had a big steamer come in to the big dock down there and we were there to meet her every Sunday. And all the people that come in on her headed for the beach. Well, we headed for the steamer. We stayed on her all day. Everybody left her but a couple of men there, selling lemonade. But we just run all over that thing and [went] swimming off the dock, the pier, way out there in the sound. Great, big old Vansciver. She was a big old boat."

Boone Tillett recalled of the Sunday steamers, "When we were little boys we used to go down to the steamer, the Hattie Creef. The people would walk up the pier and to the store and to their cottages. We would walk under the pier in case somebody dropped a nickel or a dime. And we would find 'em. We would go up to Aunt Mave Moore's and had her tell our fortune. Give her a nickel to tell our fortune. Oh, she'd tell us what great men we were going to be."

Some residents remember a black man who entertained visitors by dancing and playing spoons for the money people threw to him. The big bands that played on board the steamers also played at the hotel pavilion. Flat's Band, a group of black musicians who played bones, bass fiddle and kazoo, was also popular.

Residents and vacationers alike patronized the dance pavilion at the Nags Head Hotel and other hostelries. Natives and newcomers listened to music, danced, and sipped soft drinks. "I remember my sisters going [to the pavilion]," said Ester Beacham. "And I remember some of their pretty dresses. One sister had a tomato red organdy dress." The Casino was another favorite spot. Texie Tillett Meekins remembered that the Casino was "just a big open house. They propped the windows open so it was all open on the water. There was always something going there for recreation."

There were some tensions between the year 'round residents and the summer visitors but by and large natives and vacationers enjoyed cordial relations. According to Wanchese native Mildred Midgett, "I'm sure [that local people didn't mingle with summer tourists] when I was a young person going to Nags Head. You stuck with your crowd that you knew. We had absolutely nothing to do with Elizabeth City children fifty years ago. You just stuck with the ones you knew." While peddling soft-shell crabs to summer people, Evelyn Gray remembered "one woman who said she'd take 'em if I'd clean them. I went in and cleaned them for her and they never even offered me no water to wash my hands. You know, after you clean a crab, your hands are dirty. So I didn't stop at that place no more."

However, friendships sometimes developed. Alwilda Culpepper of Nags Head Woods worked as a domestic for the summer people. According to her daughter-in-law, Sylvia Culpepper, "these people liked her as their friend. Somtimes people that have as much money as some of these people down here don't do that. But, honey, they loved her as their own friends and had her right in with them. Invited her to Elizabeth City and gave her places to stay with them." Alwilda later named her son, Hal Wood Culpepper, after a summer visitor from Edenton.

In the first part of the twentieth century, the residents of Nags Head Woods were seldom at a loss for ways to have fun. Family, neighbors, and the environment itself were great sources of pleasure. But the beautiful natural scenery lured vacationers to the Outer Banks, and the tourist trade spawned new forms of commercial recreation. Today, the result is apparent.

The Snipe Hunt

A 'coon hunt turned into a snipe hunt for Norris Austin.

"One time it was a real clear fall night back in October that my Uncle Walter and I went out 'coon hunting. He had 'coon dogs that he would take out to hunt 'coons. We were up on those hills about in where the Preserve is now, and he decided that he heard some snipe calling. He had a tow sack, and he left the sack with me. Of course, I'm only seven or eight years old, maybe nine. So he leaves the bag and the lantern with me to hold. He said, 'You hold this light and bag open.' And he was going down and scare the snipe up.

"After he was gone a little while, I realized that there wasn't any snipe and that I had been had. So I put the lantern out and walked back up the road. And the cemetery was on a hill. I came up from the south end and I saw him down on the other end sitting on the side of the road. So I got behind one of the tombstones—probably one of my great-grandfathers—and I started groaning, making this real awful groan. And I saw him jump up, and he looked all around and started to sit back down and I groaned again, real hard. He took off to the house. I let him get ahead of me a little bit, then I caught up and we got to the house at the same time. He was a great tease. He never said anything about who was in the graveyard. I think we both realized who each other was."

The Coast Guard Swing

Sylvia Culpepper's account shows that there was a variety of places to dance—in the homes of neighbors, at the Coast Guard stations, or at the Casino.

"We had square dances at different people's houses, went in anybody['s house] who had enough room for it. 'Miss' Mary Wise would like to have you and she would say, 'Come on, now, we're going to have a dance.' Some of them played a little bit of string music, but Mr. Culpepper's accordion—'squeeze box'—was the most important thing at that time. I don't know where Mr. Culpepper got his accordion; he always had it. He could play 'Turkey in the Straw' and some pretty good modern ones too, like 'There's a Spinning Wheel in the Corner.' We use to dance to 'Little Old Lady Passing By' and all those. They're still pretty.

"And we had a lot of dances at the Coast Guard stations. Oh, that was the best of all. You'd see people from other places. All these Coast Guard men did the 'Coast Guard Swing,' we called it. It was different from anything you ever saw. Instead of dancing, they took you right across the floor and right back again I'm telling you, it was amazing.

"'Miss' Mary Wise's boys were young and they were good dancers. We'd get one of these Coast Guard men (they were older) and we'd wave for Jack or some of 'Miss' Mary's boys to deliver us. They'd get us going just a back step across,

ca. 1915

"I remember my sisters going [to the pavilion], and I remember some of their pretty dresses. One sister had a tomato red organdy dress."
Ester Beacham

and back again and back. We called it the 'Coast Guard Swing' [even though] these old Coast Guard men didn't know it. They thought they could dance just as good. One old man used to get me going and I thought he was going to kill himself. I'd wave for Jack to come and he'd come and tap him on the shoulder and he'd pick up somebody else. We had more fun going to those dances.

"We did the 'Big Apple' at the Casino. The 'Big Apple' is the most fun of anything in the world. You join in a circle and you'd dance . . . 'Suzie-Q' and 'Truckin' on Down.' There was all different kinds of steps you had to do. The 'Suzie-Q' was where you'd go in and out, in and out. And 'Truckin'' was where you'd shuffle your feet around. It was fun because it was all together in a circle. You were joining in with everybody.

"At the Casino they had big bands. Really, you couldn't imagine. I don't know how this guy from Manteo that owned the Casino ever got such big bands down here to this little place, but he did. They played all that Guy Lombardo music. I love it. That's my music.

"The Casino was running during the summer and during the winter at certain times. They'd open it up about Easter and then it would last until maybe the late fall. During the late fall, once in a while they'd go in there and open it up and have a special dance for the groups around here."

Leaving the Woods

The scattering of Nags Head Woods people that had begun during World War I intensified in the 1930s. Schooling, jobs, and the military drew many residents away from the Outer Banks altogether. Bad storms that battered the sound side of Bodie Island—especially the storm of 1932—prompted some to move toward the ocean. The beach highway, completed in 1931, lured others toward the Atlantic. "We thought it was going to be wonderful," Sylvia Culpepper reflected. "We were young and we thought that's what we needed to do . . . get out where everybody was going by. . . . Pretty silly." The last native to call Nags Head Woods home was Maggie Tillett, who left shortly after her husband died in 1948.

Vandelia Brown's story shows how larger historical events and family ties prompted her departure from the woods in 1929. A decade earlier, Vandelia's sister Winnie, a schoolteacher, moved to Nash County, North Carolina, to take the place of a teacher who had died during the 1918 flu epidemic. Before long, Winnie met the nephew of the folks with whom she boarded. They eventually married and started a family. Winnie asked her younger sister to come help her, and later Vandelia married the half-brother of Winnie's husband and moved to Zebulon.

Mrs. Brown still has a special place in her heart for Nags Head Woods. "I've been away fifty-six years but still love to go back, though many I grew up with are gone [and] many changes have been made. You would never know we once had a nice home and plantation there along with many other families in the early nineteen hundreds. My dad got many compliments on his homeplace, and I've never been able to pull up my roots. It is still sacred soil to me.

"Our modern generation might feel our neighborhood would be a backward people, and we did not have chance for a lot of culture as some have had. But we have found our people went out into the world and rated well. We have had some lawyers, engineers, teachers, nurses, expert carpenters, and many high-ranking servicemen who chose this profession and to me they seemed to do as well as the average. Our dialect may be different but has not been any holdback. And we may get called 'Down-the-Bankers' but this is easy to live down, and I find many folks paying big prices to go visit down there and many choose to retire and live their last years there.

"Our forty or more families have scattered far and wide, but I feel all of us love to go back when we can—to see the changes eighty years can make, and I, for one, am proud to be a transplanted 'Down-the-Banker.'"

Sylvia Culpepper still lives close to Nags Head Woods. For her, a Bible verse captures the meaning of that community. " 'And everyone helped his neighbor. And everyone said to his brother, "Be of good courage."' It's in Isaiah, and I just noticed it a lot and always thought a lot about it. 'Everyone helped his neighbor,' and that's the way we did. . . . You see, we had our own people and then . . . the 'city people' and they came down and joined in. They were just as friendly and treated us just like they were. They don't do it now as much. They sort of think you, I don't know, don't know how to read or something. But then, they loved the people in the Woods . . . and they thought we were wonderful. And we loved them, too. We were just like one big family, all of us.

"Everybody helped each other and wanted good for everybody. There wasn't any greed or any jealousy or anything like that going on. There's so much of that now that it's awful. But then, there wasn't. Everybody was glad of anything good that happened to your neighbor. We old people left, we still are. But so many people come in now that we don't know. It's getting commercialized.

"And we loved the different things—we loved the sound, we loved the ocean, we loved the dunes. And now, it's shopping and all that stuff. Of course, we did like once in a while to go shopping, but our minds weren't set on it. Nags Head to us meant the ocean and going swimming, and climbing up sand dunes and going in the Woods. That's what it first meant to me."

A SELECTION OF
SECONDARY SOURCES CONSULTED

Bishir, Catherine W., "The 'Unpainted Aristocracy': The Beach Cottages of Old Nags Head." North Carolina Historical Review, Vol 54, no. 4, October, 1977, pp. 367-392.

Dunbar, Gary. *Historical Geography of the North Carolina Outer Banks.* Coastal Studies Series Number Three, edited by Fred Kniffen. Baton Rouge: Louisiana State University Press, 1958.

Otte, Lee J., Atkinson, Deborah S., Atkinson, Timothy A. "Nags Head Woods: A Biological Inventory," Volume 2, 1984.

Outlaw, Edward R. *Old Nag's Head.* Puente, California: La Puente Valley Journal, 1952.

Stick, David. *The Outer Banks of North Carolina, 1585-1958.* Chapel Hill: The University of North Carolina Press, 1958.

Afterword

By Amy Glass and Lu Ann Jones, March 4, 2018

Almost as soon as The Nature Conservancy broached the possibility of reissuing *"Everyone Helped His Neighbor"* we reread our copies of the book. What a treat it was to recall laughing along with Sylvia Culpepper as she told us the story of "Jimmy and the Bull" and marveling at the poetry in her description of "The Twilight Haul." We remembered visiting the old Corolla Post Office where Norris Austin was postmaster—and how few people had yet discovered the beaches north of Duck. We felt like we shared the shore with Boone Tillett as he and his father were "Counting the Waves." Doing oral history interviews is a privilege.

Three things stood out as we considered the book from this distance. The first is how lives are shaped by the physical geography of our places of birth and how vividly connected the island residents of Nags Head Woods were to forest, sound, and sea. Livelihoods and pastimes depended on and were given purpose by location, a fact that is present in almost every reflection shared with us. These stories could only have happened here, and through them the land and the water protected by the ecological preserve speak to us.

Second is how, despite being bound to that place, these residents could and did access worlds beyond Nags Head Woods. Their fishing boats, ferries, and freight vessels connected them to market towns in northeastern North Carolina and to ports as far north as New York City. Thus, Woods residents themselves thoroughly and delightfully debunked the notion of an isolated and backward people that outsiders had invented and perpetuated about them.

Finally, we were grateful all over again that people had welcomed into their homes a couple of university gals toting a cassette recorder and asking a lot of questions. These unforgettable storytellers spared no detail as they eagerly recalled lives lived decades before. The landscape itself resurrected memories. We recall how Ester Tillett Beacham shyly offered us her hand-drawn map of the Woods community as she remembered it—replete with homesteads, school, churches, ponds, and dunes. The charming drawing eventually became the cover of our book.

Conducting the interviews, transcribing the tape recordings, writing the book, curating a set of photographs, and preparing the manuscript for publication offered an intense, and joyful, collaboration that lasted little more than six months. Although we remained friends, our careers followed separate paths. But we've never forgotten the stories of Nags Head Woods.

About the Authors

AMY'S STORY

Shortly after *"Everyone Helped His Neighbor"* was published, I was asked to conduct another series of oral history interviews on the Outer Banks, this time with current and former residents of Hatteras and Ocracoke Islands. The interviews for the "Lifeways of the Outer Banks" project of the National Park Service, collected in July of 1988, are part of the State Archives of North Carolina and are housed at the Outer Banks History Center in Manteo. From those interviews, I vividly remember sitting on the stoop of Ocracoke's Old Garrish House in the sweltering late afternoon July heat while Maurice Ballance and Edgar Howard played guitar and banjo and sang old-timey music, telling stories in between hearty laughter. It is thrilling to me now to revisit those treasured memories afresh, as well as the interviews Lu Ann and I heard, as *Memories of Nags Head Woods* is given a new life.

Although my career path has diverted from collecting oral histories, the lessons I learned through these coastal history projects, and my years with the Southern Oral History Program, have stayed with me and informed all of my life's adventures. After the publication of the book, I became interested in technical writing, pursued coursework in that area, and entered the burgeoning technology field in North Carolina's Research Triangle Park. Later, that interest led to a fascination with user experience design: How do people interact with technology? How do we design those interactions so the software is easy to use? Some of that work involves interviewing technology users, and there my oral history training directly affects my work. I met and married my husband, and we've raised two daughters in Durham. Community engagement is important, and I have been a volunteer and board member at the Durham Literacy Center, served on several PTAs, and now sing with the Women's Voices Chorus of Chapel Hill.

LU ANN'S STORY

In the past thirty years I have held a number of jobs, and oral history has remained central to all of them. By the time *"Everyone Helped His Neighbor"* appeared, I was beginning the most ambitious project of my career. *An Oral History of Southern Agriculture*, supported for five years by the Smithsonian Institution, allowed me to document changes in the rural South by interviewing the men and women who had witnessed and initiated those changes. During field trips in eight states, some two hundred narrators described the transition from mules to machinery, the coming of electricity, and the drastic decline in the number of farmers. Like the last residents of Nags Head Woods, this generation of rural elders knew they were among the last witnesses to a vanished way of life and were keen to tell their stories.

Between 1991 and today, I have toggled between academic and public history work. In 1996 I completed my doctorate at the University of North Carolina at

Chapel Hill; the southern agriculture oral histories were at the center of my dissertation and the book *Mama Learned Us to Work: Farm Women in the New South*, published by UNC Press in 2002. I taught oral history and other courses at East Carolina University and the University of South Florida until 2009, when I became a historian with the National Park Service in Washington, DC. Today my interviews still revolve around people and place as I record the stories of our public lands stewards. Although my husband and I have not lived in North Carolina for several years, our hearts are there every day.

◇◇◇◇◇◇◇

"Everyone Helped His Neighbor" reminds us that oral history interviews are like good investments—they only grow more valuable over time. We believe that these stories will continue to resonate with future generations, for not only do they describe particular lifeways that have disappeared but they also remind us of universal truths that endure—no matter where we call home, deep connection with family, friends, and neighbors sustains us.